Whistles and Wedding Rings

Devotions for Coaches and Spouses

Roger D. Lipe

WHISTLES AND WEDDING RINGS

Cross Training Publishing
www.crosstrainingpublishing.com
(308) 293-3891
Copyright © 2017 by Roger D. Lipe
ISBN: 978-1-938254-70-3

Unless otherwise noted, all Scriptures are from the Holy Bible, New Living Translation, copyright © 1996, 2004, 2015 by Tyndale House Foundation. Used by permission of Tyndale House Publishers Inc., Carol Stream, Illinois 60188. All rights reserved.

Back cover photo credit: Byron Hetzler

No part of this book may be reproduced without written permission from the publisher, except by a reviewer who may quote brief passages in a review; nor may any part of this book be reproduced, stored in a retrieval system or transmitted in any form or other without written permission from the publisher.

Foreword

Home-field advantage is very real in the sports culture. We all want to go undefeated at home. If your marriage is to survive the time, financial and pressure demands that coaching brings then winning must begin at home. Your home. Few marriages are in the crosshairs of Satan more than coaches. **Whistles and Weddings Rings** will help any coach and their spouse stay connected to Christ and each other by helping create healthy conversation around the things that matter. We must be good on offense and defense to win at our marriages, and this book will help you in both. Win at Home!

Shane Williamson
President and CEO
Fellowship of Christian Athletes

Introduction

Whistles and wedding rings are words that immediately evoke pictures in our minds emblematic of coaching and family life. Most people would not couple them this way, but they are tightly linked for coaching families.

This book contains two series of devotional thoughts specifically written for coaches and their spouses. The first lists several important qualities to a coaching family's life—respect, devotion, loyalty, sacrifice, and intimacy. The second set builds on a baseball concept of being a five tool player. A five tool baseball player can run, throw, field, hit for power, and hit for average. We will use these skills as metaphors for coaching families.

We understand the very busy nature of your lives, therefore the thoughts are brief and direct. They are designed so that you may read them separately or together as a couple. There are questions at the end of each day's reading for private contemplation or discussion.

Thanks to the following people who contributed to the process of composition and editing: Robbie Gwinn, Daniel Chappell, Julie Martin, numerous coaches and Fellowship of Christian Athletes staff people, my mentor and friend Fred Bishop, and Bruce and Diane Pruellage for the solitude of their lake house.

Understanding, Honoring, Coheirs of Grace
Respect
Day 1
1 Peter 3:7

How do coaches, competitors, and sports officials demonstrate respect for each other? How is one's experience in sport affected by such expressions of respect? How should a coach show proper respect for his or her spouse? How should that relationship be affected by consistent displays of genuine respect or honor?

The Apostle Peter wrote about such matters in chapter three, verse seven of his first letter to his friends. There it reads "Husbands, in the same way, live with your wives with an understanding of their weaker nature yet showing them honor as coheirs of the grace of life, so that your prayers will not be hindered." You may already be bristling at the thought of a wife having a weaker nature, but don't let that throw you off course.

Whether a coach is male or female, whether the spouse is female or male, to consistently demonstrate respect, to communicate honor, and to treat each other as coheirs of the grace of life as a coaching family is at the heart of a thriving relationship.

A life in coaching will certainly require a good deal of understanding from your spouse. The demands of time, the pressure to win, the emotional strain, and the layers of relationship required for excellence are consuming for all concerned. To show proper honor to one's spouse will not only enhance the relationship, but this scripture says it also protects the effectiveness of our prayers.

Commit yourselves to being a coaching family that demonstrates the highest levels of respect and honor as you live together as coheirs of the grace of life.

Questions for Contemplation and Discussion:

1. How do the coaches, competitors, and sports officials you know demonstrate respect for each other? How well do they show respect for and honor their spouses?
2. What are your favorite ways to express honor for your spouse? How does he or she respond?
3. How could receiving grace for life from Christ, with your spouse, shape your life of prayer and help you build a coaching family characterized by respect and honor?

Living with Humility, Gentleness, and Patience
Respect
Day 2
Ephesians 4:1-2

How does a Christ-honoring coaching family live with respect at the center of their relationship? What sorts of character traits spring from such an attitude as they live together and love each other?

In the Apostle Paul's letter to the Ephesians, he challenged his friends with these words, "Therefore I, the prisoner for the Lord, urge you to walk worthy of the calling you have received, with all humility and gentleness, with patience, accepting one another in love…" As he wrote from prison, Paul called his friends to demonstrate respect for each other in layers of loving attitudes.

Think about how sport would be transformed if everyone demonstrated humility, gentleness, patience, acceptance, and love. Think about how your coaching family would be if you each lived with these traits in full bloom.

To show respect to one's coaching colleagues, even to one's most bitter coaching rivals, elevates the nature of the sport and brings out the best in all concerned. That is also true in coaching families. When we live worthy of our calling in

Christ, we will be humble, gentle, patient, and accepting of one another.

Today's challenge is simply to live in keeping with the noble nature of our calling. Demonstrate respect for your spouse before, during, and after practice. Be humble and gentle during pregame, during the contest, and after the competition is over. Live patiently and acceptingly with each other whether the season is graced by wins or plagued by losses.

Questions for Contemplation and Discussion:

1. How does a Christ-honoring coaching family live with respect at the center of their husband/wife relationship?
2. What are some ways your spouse demonstrates respect for you? How do you show honor to your spouse when in the public eye?
3. How can you, as a coaching family, walk in a manner worthy of your calling in Christ? List some ways to demonstrate each of these:
    a. Humility
    b. Gentleness
    c. Patience
    d. Acceptance

Love is the Game Plan
Respect
Day 3
1 Corinthians 16:13-14

Coaches constantly evaluate, analyze, time, score, and measure all the processes and results of their lives in sport. How well do the coaches you know evaluate their relationships with their spouses? If you were to give your spouse a score for acting in love (1 being rarely, 10 being always), what number would you assign? You may not want to say that number out loud just now. What score would you give yourself?

In the Apostle Paul's first letter to his friends in Corinth, Greece, he wrote, "Be on guard. Stand firm in the faith. Be courageous. Be strong. And do everything with love." These four directives inform our lives in coaching on a number of fronts. Not the least of them is the relationship we have with our spouses. Surely a life long love relationship will require being on guard, standing firm, courage, strength, and a commitment to constantly acting in love.

The hustle and anxiety that accompanies a life in sport can tear at our margins and lead us to doing most things in love, but slipping into doing some things rather selfishly. Our society seems to war against us as it chides us to demand our individual rights and exert independence.

The challenge here is to hear these directives from Paul in a plural sense. We must be on guard as a couple. We will stand firm in the faith as a family. We will be courageous as husband and wife. We are to be strong together. We will do everything in love for each other.

Today's game plan is simple; do everything in love. That starts with a healthy respect for our spouse and extends to all the others we encounter in this day. Coaching family, be on guard. Stand firm in the faith, be courageous, be strong, and do everything in love.

Questions for Contemplation and Discussion:

1. Coach, what are the elements of sport that you evaluate, analyze, time, and score?
2. Coach and spouse, what are the elements of your relationship you would give the highest scores? Which would receive the lowest scores?
    a. Respect?
    b. Communication?
    c. Time together?
    d. Intimacy?
    e. Loyalty?
    f. Common interests?
3. What is your game plan for putting away selfish living to prefer doing everything in love?

Kind, Tenderhearted Forgiveness
Respect
Day 4
Ephesians 4:32

Think about the coaching families in your life who are kind and tenderhearted, quick to forgive. How much do you respect them? How well do you and your family demonstrate those same qualities? What makes some people able to forgive, to extend kindness and compassion, while others seem to be consumed by envy, selfish motives and hold grudges? The scripture has some insight for us into the transforming nature of God's forgiveness.

Paul, the Apostle, in writing to his friends in Ephesus said "Instead, be kind to each other, tenderhearted, forgiving one another, just as God through Christ has forgiven you." The power for living out the first part of this verse is found in its final phrase.

The power to push past our natural and selfish desires to prefer kindness toward our spouses is found in the forgiveness given by God through Christ. To be tenderhearted rather than hard-hearted is surely the result of a forgiven heart. To appropriate the forgiveness we have received from God through Christ is the only way we can quickly forgive those who hurt us.

Every coach and every spouse could make a long list of offenses that need to be forgiven. We would all have to plead guilty to a bottomless pit of selfish acts toward our spouses. The great news here is that we can extend the forgiveness we have received from God. Rather than our relationships being plagued by guilt, pain and regret, they can be rich with forgiveness, grace, and mercy.

Paul's challenge to us is to push back against the normal way of the world, to prefer kindness to being mean. He calls us to be tenderhearted rather than cynical and faultfinding. We're implored to quickly forgive instead of forever holding grudges.

Questions for Contemplation and Discussion:

1. Who are some of the coaching families you know that demonstrate kindness, tender hearts and are quick to forgive? How do they do that?
2. What are some consequences of holding grudges, living selfishly, and refusing to forgive?
3. Take a moment to think about something for which you need to ask forgiveness of your spouse. How and when will you ask for forgiveness?
4. How quick are you to forgive others? Give yourself a letter grade (A = Wow, that was quick, F = Wow, will you ever forgive?).

Two are Better than One
Respect
Day 5
Ecclesiastes 4:9-12

Coach, in what ways are your colleagues complementary to your coaching? Is it their personalities, their coaching style, their age, experience, or something else? How does your spouse make your life more complete? How would your life be lesser without your coaching spouse? How does the Lord Jesus' presence strengthen your coaching family's bond?

The book of Hebrew poetry titled Ecclesiastes includes these insightful thoughts in chapter four and verses nine through twelve. "Two people are better off than one, for they can help each other succeed. If one person falls, the other can reach out and help. But someone who falls alone is in real trouble. Likewise, two people lying close together can keep other warm. But how can one be warm alone? A person standing alone can be attacked and defeated, but two can stand back-to-back and conquer. Three are even better, for a triple-braided cord is not easily broken."

This writer had certainly observed successful teams and strong marriages. Both require commitment, between teammates or spouses, to pursue excellence, to provide security, and to give each other comfort. A life in sport often feels like the coaching staff is standing together, back-to-back, taking on all comers.

Sometimes it may even feel like coach and spouse are standing back-to-back, battling all the forces that war against their family and even threaten their relationship as husband and wife. This text says we are much stronger together than either would be separately. As our coaching staffs are made up of complementary personalities and gift sets, so our families are gifted with a marvelously diverse set of men, women, and children who make our lives more complete. We would be much lesser if any one of them was missing.

One final encouragement is found hiding in the final sentence. After speaking of two people and the power of their bond, the author suddenly speaks of a triple-braided cord and a third person. This third person in the cord of relational bond between a husband and wife is the Spirit of God. He bonds our hearts together in divine love, grace, and mercy. Our relationship is infinitely stronger because of His transformational power.

Questions for Contemplation and Discussion:

1. How do your friends and colleagues in coaching enhance your life and family?
2. What are the particular strengths your spouse brings to your marriage? Feel free to tell him or her about them.
3. When and how do you sense the transforming presence of God's Spirit in your marriage and family?

Honor and Affection
Devotion
Day 1
Romans 12:10

Across your career in coaching, who has loved you like you were family? How do the people in your coaching family express genuine affection? Are you huggers and kissers or more the fist bump and high five variety? Who is there in your coaching network that would be instantly honored if he or she was to walk into the room?

As he wrote to his friends in Rome, the Apostle Paul spoke of such matters. These words are recorded in chapter twelve, verse ten. "Love each other with genuine affection, and take delight in honoring each other." Depending upon the family culture in which you grew up, you probably find one of these really easy but the other more difficult.

Some cultures are strong at displaying affection; they hug, kiss, and otherwise express their love for each other very freely. Others take a more subdued, stoic and subtle approach to how they demonstrate their love. Remarkably, many couples are made up of people with opposite expressions of affection and that takes some time to work through.

Some families and coaching staffs are strong at displaying honor for those they respect and love. They will speak glowingly of the ones who represent the team or the family well. There are also strong and loving coaches and families who play things a little more closely to the vest. They expect people to do well, and when they succeed, they have simply met their expectations. Praise and honor are not simply cast about so liberally.

The Apostle challenges us to push through our cultural boundaries and approach the expression of love and honor with purpose and conviction. Make it a point to love your spouse and family with genuine affection, whether you find it easy or not. Set out to honor your spouse at every opportunity, even when it seems they are just meeting expectations.

Questions for Contemplation and Discussion:

1. What is your favorite way to express genuine affection for your spouse?
2. What is your spouse's favorite way to receive your genuine affection? (If you don't know, now is the perfect time to ask.)
3. List three ways you can honor your spouse today. Write them down here.

    a. _____
    b. _____
    c. _____

Unified in Mind and Purpose
Devotion
Day 2
Philippians 2:1-2

Think about a time in the life of your coaching family when unity, loyalty, and absolute devotion were needed to overcome adversity. How did those qualities in your team, or the lack of them, affect the outcome? Are these character traits more evident in you on the field of competition or in your family's life away from sport? These are tough questions, but they lead to some strong encouragement.

As he wrote to his friends in a town called Philippi, the Apostle Paul said this in chapter two, verses one and two, "Is there any encouragement from belonging to Christ? Any comfort from his love? Any fellowship together in the Spirit? Are your hearts tender and compassionate? Then make me truly happy by agreeing wholeheartedly with each other, loving one another and working together with one mind and purpose."

Paul called his friends to agree wholeheartedly, to love one another, and to work together with unified mind and purpose. That sounds like what a wise coach would call a team to do. What separates Paul from most of the coaches we know is the power behind his impassioned plea.

He directly ties his friends' agreement, love, and unified work to the encouragement, comfort, fellowship, and life transformation they have received from Christ Jesus. This is the source of such life-giving character. Nothing else can accomplish such a feat.

Our challenge is the same. In our coaching lives, in our family lives, in every facet of life, we are wonderfully empowered by the living God to demonstrate love, compassion, unity, singularity of mind and purpose with those we love and serve. Let's make the Apostle and the Lord Jesus truly happy by building teams and families that are full of such character.

Questions for Contemplation and Discussion:

1. How happy does it make you to see your team or your family agreeing wholeheartedly, loving one another and working together in a unified way? Tell your spouse about that.
2. Whose face do you see in your head when you read Philippians 2:1-2?
3. What would be the best way to contact one or two of those people today to thank them for their influence in your life and family? Make it happen.

Love is Sticky
Devotion
Day 3
Colossians 3:14

Has your coaching family ever been connected with a program marked by unity and love? If so, it must have been fantastic. If not, do you believe that can be achieved? Do you find everyone in the coaching community easy to love, or have there been some challenging times with certain people? How would making the purposeful choice to love develop a perfect bond of unity in your coaching family?

This is precisely the point made by the Apostle Paul as he wrote to his friends in the church at Colossae in chapter three, verse fourteen, "Above all, clothe yourselves with love, which binds us all together in perfect harmony." It seems pretty simple until you have to love some unlovely or seemingly unlovable people. Some coaching staffs and most families have some of each.

The language Paul uses is very important to this process. He says, "Above all." What follows is obviously of greatest importance. It's like when the coach blows the whistle to get everyone's attention. Consider the whistle blown. "Clothe yourselves with love." To wrap ourselves in love is to be done as purposefully and as regularly as we put on clothes to start each day. Such love is the stuff that "binds us all together in perfect harmony." This love, purposefully put on, is the sticky stuff that binds teams, coaching staffs, marriages, families, and friends together.

Coaching family, above all, wrap yourselves in the wonderfully sticky love of God. It will bind you together. It will keep you unified perfectly. Put it on today, tomorrow, the next day, and so on. This is the substance of life-long devotion.

Questions for Contemplation and Discussion:

1. Think about the coaches and families you know who are characterized by unity and love.
2. What makes them tick? How do they clothe themselves with love?
3. What are some daily habits you can cultivate that help you put on love, purposefully and regularly?

Living in Love
Devotion
Day 4
1 John 4:16

How would knowing that the head coach, the athletic director, or the club owner was 100 percent devoted to you and your family affect your approach to coaching? One would assume it would lead to an amazing level of confidence and an absence of anxiety. Devotion like that comes from the trust developed between people. Such trust is also developed by people as they grow in their relationships with God.

The Apostle John, when writing the first letter to his friends in chapter four, verse sixteen says, "We know how much God loves us, and we have put our trust in his love. God is love and all who live in love live in God, and God lives in them." The expression of "living in God, and God living in us" is not common to our culture and surely not to sport culture.

We can think of it in terms more familiar to sportspeople if we say, "That guy eats, drinks, sleeps, and breathes his sport." You have probably heard of coaches who would sleep at their offices on a couch, rather than go home after a long night of watching game film. That coach is "living in sport and the sport is living in him or her."

As devoted to sport as you may be, I hope you can trust the love of God and can grasp that He is in you, and you are in Him. He is even more devoted to you than you can imagine. Your spouse is devoted to you in the same way. Your hearts are inextricably entwined by the vows taken on your wedding day. The Lord Himself is the bonding agent in your relationship. He is in you, collectively, and you two are in Him, together.

Be devoted together as a coaching family. Put your trust in each other and in the Lord Jesus. Live in love, and live in God. His devotion to your family is woven into the fabric of your very souls.

Questions for Contemplation and Discussion:

1. On a 1 to 10 scale (1 is weak, 10 is super strong), how would you rate the devotion you feel from those who have the power to dismiss you from your coaching position?
2. How strongly do you feel the love of God, day to day? When do you sense it most strongly?
3. When do you most powerfully sense that God's love is binding you with your spouse?

Seals, Death, Fire, Rivers, and Fools
Devotion
Day 5
Song of Songs 8:6-7

What metaphors or figures of speech would you use to describe the level of devotion experienced in your coaching family? Would you say it's as strong as a shot putter? Could it be as powerful as a nose tackle? Maybe it's as flimsy as a swimmer's racing suit or maybe permanent like a tattoo. The Bible is full of rich metaphors, and today we'll read some related to devotion.

King Solomon expressed his devotion beautifully in the book Song of Songs, in chapter 8, verses six and seven. There it reads, "Place me like a seal over your heart, like a seal on your arm. For love is as strong as death, its jealousy as enduring as the grave. Love flashes like fire, the brightest kind of flame. Many waters cannot quench love, nor can rivers drown it. If a man tried to buy love with all his wealth, his offer would be utterly scorned." Love is likened to a seal, to death, the grave, fire, water, rivers, and a treasure of unimaginable worth.

Like a seal over one's heart or bound to one's arm, like the wedding band on your finger, love bears the mark of the person to whom we are devoted. As strong as death and as permanent as the grave is the devoted love one has for his or her spouse. Love burns hot and bright between lovers who are bound together for life, and the mightiest rivers could never quench its flames. Only a scornful fool would presume to buy such a priceless jewel as devoted love.

Whether you feel the emotions of such expression, this is the true nature of the love God is growing in your marriage. Commit yourself to your spouse through the unquenchable fire of devotion. Your vows of love and fidelity to your spouse are a seal stronger than death, the grave, fire, or water. Trust the Lord Jesus to fan the flames of passion for your spouse today.

Questions for Contemplation and Discussion:

1. What is a metaphor or simile that describes your devotion to your spouse today?
2. Take a moment to recall the day you received your wedding ring. Has your devotion to your spouse grown or diminished since that day?
3. What are the places, activities, and situations that bring out the best in your spouse? Be sure to share those thoughts with him or her today. That's the stuff that fans flames of passionate devotion.

'Til Death Do Us Part
Loyalty
Day 1
Ruth 1:16-17

Who have been the most loyal people in your lives as a coaching family? Take a moment to recall their faces, their hearts, and the situations that revealed their loyalty. How did they verbalize or demonstrate their loyalty to you? How did you respond? Today we'll read a remarkable expression of loyalty between two remarkable people.

In the book of Hebrew history Ruth, tells this wonderful story, and in chapter one, verses sixteen and seventeen we read, "But Ruth replied, 'Don't ask me to leave you and turn back. Wherever you go, I will go; wherever you live, I will live. Your people will be my people, and your God will be my God. Wherever you die, I will die, and there I will be buried. May the lord punish me severely if I allow anything but death to separate us.'" Ruth made this stunning statement of loyalty to her mother-in-law, Naomi, after they had both been widowed.

The normal course of things would have been for Ruth to return to her native land, remarry and carry on. Her remarkable loyalty to Naomi would not take this easier way out but required that she stay with her mother-in-law, care for her and commit to her until death would separate them.

Loyalty is an immensely valuable commodity in the world of coaching. It also seems to become rarer from year to year. To maintain one's loyalty in the face of critical fans, demanding players' parents, foolish media, and disloyal colleagues is both uncommon and tremendously important. That is just as true for the coach's spouse and family sitting in the seats as it is in the coach's office.

Our challenge is to commit to loyalty in the same way as Ruth committed to Naomi. She was in for the long haul. She would not be deterred by anything less than death. Such loyalty is rewarded with loyalty, trust, and love. Ruth's loyalty is honored by the Lord God as she marries a man named Boaz, becomes the grandmother of King David, and is one of four women mentioned in Matthew's account of Jesus' family heritage.

Questions for Contemplation and Discussion:

1. Take a moment to recall a situation that required loyalty from you toward a coaching colleague or family member.
2. From where did that loyalty come? How did it affect your relationship?
3. For whom are you now demonstrating loyalty that will shape the lives of others?

Humble and Gentle?
Loyalty
Day 2
Ephesians 4:2-3

Think about a team or coaching family you know that has a unifying sense of peace and love. How can that possibly happen when coaching a competitive sport is your family business? What could we build into our families to ensure that our bond of loyalty is strong and enduring? The Bible is a limitless supply of wise instruction for this process.

In writing to his friend in Ephesus, the Apostle Paul was very direct in his language in chapter four, verses two and three. There it says, "Always be humble and gentle. Be patient with each other, making allowance for each other's faults because of your love. Make every effort to keep yourselves united in the Spirit, binding yourselves together with peace."

It would seem that Paul knew very few coaches, as his first directive is to, "Always be humble and gentle." How many coaches do you know who are described as always humble and gentle? Thinking more directly about your coaching family, would you describe your relationships as being full of humility and gentleness? Are you patient with each other? Are you mindful of your love while you are overlooking each others' faults? Does your coaching family keep itself together by being united in the Spirit of Christ Jesus? You're probably doing better than you first thought.

In our coaching and family relationships, we can surely make every effort to keep ourselves united in the Spirit. We can be bound together with peace. Peace is enhanced as we act humbly, gently, and patiently toward each other. Loyalty springs from such relationships, but it doesn't fall on us. It's our responsibility to make every Spirit-led effort.

Questions for Contemplation and Discussion:

1. How does your coaching family work to maintain loyalty? How well is that working?
2. Coach, give yourself a score (1 is horrible, 10 is outstanding), on how humble and gentle you are with your coaching peers. How would you score yourself with your family?
3. In what ways will you make the effort to keep your coaching family united in the Spirit this week?

Love is… Love is not…
Loyalty
Day 3
1 Corinthians 13:4-5

When has your life in coaching required patience and kindness? How did that situation challenge your loyalty to others in and around your coaching family? Can you recall the destructive influence of jealous, rude, boastful, and proud people? What sorts of situations make people in your coaching family irritable and lead them to keep a score of offenses? It seems these situations are not peculiar to the coaching community, as they are mentioned often in the Bible.

The Apostle Paul wrote to his friends in Corinth, Greece with these remarks in chapter thirteen, verses four and five, "Love is patient and kind. Love is not jealous or boastful or proud or rude. It does not demand its own way. It is not irritable, and it keeps no record of being wronged." Paul's friends needed clear descriptions as to what love is and what it is not. I would imagine each of us could also use a reminder.

Loyalty in a coaching staff or a family is more easily accomplished when we treat each other patiently and kindly; that is what love is. When we put away jealousy, boasting, pride, and rudeness, love and loyalty flourish. Instead of demanding our way, being grumpy, and keeping a scorecard of times we're offended, let's choose to love our colleagues and family.

Our lives in sport bring with them strong challenges to our love and loyalty. Putting on patience and kindness like our coaching gear fights against the forces that tear at our relationships. Guarding our attitudes from jealousy and pride will make us much better spouses. Being quick to forgive instead of irritable and fault finding make us much more pleasant people with whom to live. If you want loyalty from those in your coaching family, lead with love, patience and kindness.

Questions for Contemplation and Discussion:

1. Take a moment to recall a situation that challenged your loyalty to someone. How did you express your loyalty?
2. How have your coaching colleagues or family members demonstrated loyalty to you? Take some time today to thank them.
3. What is your game plan for putting on patience and kindness as you lead your team and your family?

Unquenchable Love
Loyalty
Day 4
Song of Songs 8:7

What are some challenges to loyalty that regularly occur during your life in coaching? When have you been tempted with thoughts of the next career move or replacing an obviously inferior head coach? How did those thoughts assault your sense of loyalty to your colleagues and athletes? How has your loyalty endured these thieving thoughts?

King Solomon was a man with immeasurable wealth, as well as hundreds of wives and concubines. Many of these relationships were formed as political alliances, making for clumsy situations and divided loyalties. He wrote in Song of Songs about the power of true love. There it reads, "Many waters cannot quench love, nor can rivers drown it. If a man tried to buy love with all his wealth, his offer would be utterly scorned." He certainly knew about buying things, but he also knew that love was beyond purchase.

Love is the real power in loyalty. Love-fueled loyalty cannot be quenched and whole rivers of water cannot drown it. The loyalty held by coaching colleagues, family, and friends can never be bought, and the wealthy fool who would try to buy it will be sent away in scornful shame.

Our challenge as coaching families is to build our loyalty to the depths described by Solomon. That will not be done quickly, nor will it be easy. Such loyalty is tested by small matters of inconvenience, familiarity, and preference long before its power is exposed by impressive titles, long-term contracts, and prestige.

Questions for Contemplation and Discussion:

1. Take a moment to recall the most recent challenge to your loyalty. How did you respond? Are you happy with your response?
2. What are some factors that could quench the loyalty of people around your coaching family?
3. What about the loyalty you have experienced from others is beyond any amount of money?

Most Important of All…
Loyalty
Day 5
1 Peter 4:8

Think for a moment about one of the situations in your coaching career that demanded fierce and unquestioned loyalty from you. How did you maintain such loyalty in spite of the difficult circumstances? You are probably picturing in your mind people who stretch your loyalty to its limits. How long are you supposed to put up with their nonsense? Where will you find the strength of will to get through their next episode? Jesus had days and people like that on his team and in his family as well.

In his first letter to his friends of the Church in present day Turkey, the Apostle Peter wrote these words in chapter four, verse eight, "Most important of all, continue to show deep love for each other, for love covers a multitude of sins." I imagine that when Peter is penning these thoughts, he can see the Lord Jesus' face in his mind. Peter was very conscious of his multitude of sins, and he had experienced the deep love and loyalty of Jesus. Of all the disciples, it must have required immense patience and loyalty to deal with Peter for three years.

Peter emphasizes that love is the power behind loyalty as he says, "Most important of all…" Deep love for each other is the substance of loyalty in a team, in a family, between a husband and wife, as deep love carries loyalty in its arms. The depth of this love is indicated by its effect as Peter writes, "for love covers a multitude of sins." We're more than happy to have Jesus' love cover our multitude of sins, but in this verse he's referring to the multitude of sins committed by those around us.

Sometimes we're on the blunt end of the sins committed by our players, our coaching colleagues, and even our spouses. Suddenly the depth of love required seems greater and the multitude of sins is accompanied by deeply painful memories. This is why it says, "Most important of all…"

The challenge for us today, with our teams, our families, our spouses, and our coaching colleagues is to appropriate the infinitely deep love of Jesus to the multitude of sins that have been visited upon us. As we have received Jesus' love and forgiveness, we can now extend it to others. The result of such love is an enduring loyalty.

Questions for Contemplation and Discussion:

1. Who are the people and situations that push your loyalty to the breaking point?
2. How easy is it to love these people, when you just want to escape?
3. Think of some concrete ways you can appropriate the deep love of Jesus and express it toward the people who are stressing your loyalty.

Husbands, Love Your Wives
Sacrifice
Day 1
Ephesians 5:25

What are some of the sacrifices you have made to be a coaching family? Take a moment and make a list in your mind. How have you, as a husband, made sacrifices for your wife? How have you, as a wife, expressed respect for your husband's sacrifices? Why do you suppose it was God's plan for Jesus to make his life the ultimate sacrifice for us? The Bible speaks directly to such matters and informs our lives as coaching families.

Paul the Apostle wrote a letter to the church in Ephesus, and in chapter five, verse twenty-five it says, "For husbands this means love your wives, just as Christ loved the church. He gave up his life for her to make her holy and clean, washed by the cleansing of God's word." You'll notice he does not tell wives to love this way, just husbands.

Contemplate for a moment what Jesus gave up to love the church. The Creator of the universe took on human flesh. He experienced the weakness of infancy, the wonder of childhood, the awkwardness of adolescence, the confusion of adulthood, the physical pain and fatigue of humanity, and ultimately bore our sin and rebellion on the cross. That is real sacrifice of the greatest order.

By comparison, the sacrifices husbands make for their wives may seem trivial. They are, however, real and significant. When a coaching husband chooses a position based on his wife's best interest instead of his own ambition, that is sacrifice. When a husband makes a lateral or downward career move to accommodate his coaching wife's career advancement, that is genuine, loving sacrifice. When husbands seek the best for their wives and family over their own interests, that is Christ-like love.

Men, let's accept Paul's challenge and love our brides sacrificially. Your wife, like Christ's Bride the Church, is worth it.

Questions for Contemplation and Discussion:

1. Which of the sacrifices from your coaching career has been most costly?
2. Which of the sacrifices you have made for your family has been most rewarding?
3. What are some sacrifices yet to be made that you anticipate on the horizon for your coaching family?

Loving the Unworthy and Undeserving
Sacrifice
Day 2
Romans 5:8

How do you as a coaching family demonstrate your love for the people you coach? How do you show your love for the men and women with whom you coach? What does it cost you to love in such ways? Take a moment to contemplate these expressions of love and the effect they have in the lives of all concerned. This is the very work of God in your life.

In writing to his friends in Rome, the Apostle Paul penned these words in chapter five, verse eight, "But God showed his great love for us by sending Christ to die for us while we were still sinners." When we sacrificially love the people in and around our coaching family, we are joining God in his eternal mission of restoring people to relationship with himself.

We must note that it was "while we were still sinners" that Jesus came to die for us. God's way is to seek out the rebellious and wayward for relationship, rather than waiting for them to get their stuff together and then loving them. We will surely have to love the rebellious and wayward in a sacrificial manner to be similarly redemptive.

Our minds may find it easier to think of those we coach as

we think about sacrificial love and redemptive relationships, but this surely occurs at home as well. Imagine the depth of impact that will be made when a husband lays down his life for his bride. Contemplate the power of a wife's sacrificial love toward her husband. Further, think about the generational effect of a Christian coaching family on a community.

This impact, power, and generational effect only occurs in an atmosphere of sacrificial love that pursues the unworthy and undeserving. Can you be that kind of coaching family? Will you commit to being that sort of husband? Are you a wife who can show God's great love to the rebellious and foolish? By the grace of God, you can be. By the power of God, you will.

Questions for Contemplation and Discussion:

1. What are your most common demonstrations of love for the people you coach?
2. How does your coaching family show your love for your coaching colleagues?
3. What are the situations in your family that require sacrificial love? How will you pursue those who need such love?

Answering the Critics and the Curious
Sacrifice
Day 3
1 Peter 3:15-16

When has your commitment to Christ as a coaching family cost you an opportunity, a promotion, or caused you to suffer some ridicule and alienation? Are you sometimes misunderstood by your peers due to your faithful convictions? How do you explain yourself when people ask about your priorities and values? The Bible speaks directly to this sort of dilemma with strong encouragement.

In his first letter, the Apostle Peter in chapter three, verses fifteen and sixteen, wrote these words, "Instead, you must worship Christ as Lord of your life. And if someone asks about your hope as a believer, always be ready to explain it. But do this in a gentle and respectful way. Keep your conscience clear. Then if people speak against you, they will be ashamed when they see what a good life you live because you belong to Christ." Peter spent a great deal of his time being misunderstood and cutting against the grain of local culture. He was a very Jewish man living in a very gentile community.

I would imagine that as Peter visited communities during his service of the early church, he would have made his way to the sea shore and visited with fishermen. He was just like coaches who seem to always find their way to the gym, the pool, or the practice field wherever they travel. It would have been an everyday occurrence for him to answer questions about his faith and his peculiar way of living.

Your coaching family, your values and practices are no doubt a little peculiar to those in the broader coaching community. How do you answer people when they ask you about them? Peter's counsel is to do it gently and respectfully. Some will surely misunderstand, and it may cost you to hold to your convictions. It surely cost Peter greatly to hold to his. There will be sacrifices to be made in living as a Christian coaching family. They are worth it.

Questions for Contemplation and Discussion:

1. How strong is the sting of sacrifice you have made to hold on to your values for coaching? Give the pain a score (1 is "what pain?" and 10 is excruciating).
2. When have you been asked about your peculiar values by people in your coaching community? How did you answer them?
3. What are the practices of your coaching family that may bring some opposition or misunderstanding in the future? How will you plan to answer your critics?

Love Deeply with All Your Heart
Sacrifice
Day 4
I Peter 1:22

Which situations in your coaching life have refined or purified your motivation for coaching? How did those seasons affect your marriage and your family? Sometimes it's the stress and intensity of conflict that clarifies our vision and refines our motives. It's always been God's way for our lives to be purified by heat and pressure.

Peter, Jesus' disciple and one of the most important leaders of the early church, wrote these words in chapter one, verse 22 of his first letter, "You were cleansed from your sins when you obeyed the truth, so now you must show sincere love to each other as brothers and sisters. Love each other deeply with all your heart." With all our hearts, huh? Some of the people around us are not all that loveable. This is a strong challenge.

Thankfully, Peter's call to sacrificial love is tied directly to a power source. The grace to love others as brothers and sisters is linked to our having been cleansed from our sins when we obeyed the truth; that is to trust Jesus as Lord and Savior. In our natural selves, we do not possess the power to embrace the abrasive and obnoxious people around us like family, but in Christ we can and we will.

This kind of sacrificial love is expressed on the home front as well as in the coaching world. To love each other deeply with all our hearts is sometimes a challenge between spouses and their children, not to mention in-laws and extended family. Think about your crazy uncle or your spouse's bossy aunt.

The Lord's call and our privilege is to, "show sincere love to each other as brothers and sisters. Love each other deeply with all your heart." Let's get after that today.

Questions for Contemplation and Discussion:

1. Think a moment about the situations that clarified your calling to be a Christian coaching family. What were the key values and who were the key people to that calling?
2. Who has loved you like brothers and sisters along your coaching career? Take some time today to say thank you.
3. Think of three ways you can express deep, heart felt love for your spouse today. Write them here.
   a. _____
   b. _____
   c. _____

You Now Have Authority Over My Body
Sacrifice
Day 5
1 Corinthians 7:4

Which sections of the calendar are most costly to you and most challenging to your coaching family? How do you deal with the sacrificial elements of marriage in a coaching family? How do coaching couples overcome the perceived robbery of time, the constant distractions, and other challenges to relational intimacy?

In writing to his friends in Corinth, Greece, the Apostle Paul gave this counsel in chapter seven, verse four, "The wife gives authority over her body to her husband, and the husband gives authority over his body to his wife." This idea flips the normal power structure of marriage on its head. Rather than demanding our rights, Paul instructs us to give the authority for our bodies to our spouses.

You are probably thinking about sex, but this goes far beyond that. Think about all that your spouse sacrifices during any season of coaching. Both of you sacrifice large blocks of time together, sleep, healthy nutrition, children's activities, dinners at home, vacations, long weekends away, and mornings to sleep in and hold each other tightly. Some are foolishly sacrificed, but others are certainly necessary.

The big idea is to cede authority for your body to your

spouse. When she needs your presence in the house to fix something, be there. When he needs your touch and affection, give it. When she needs your attention and intimate communication, be fully present. When he needs you to simply be in the room so his world feels normal, trust him in the silence. You have given your spouse authority over your body for whatever the other needs.

It will be a sacrifice to give up your authority. It will be worth every moment of discomfort, inconvenience, and confusion, though, because the result is a deeper, more intimate relationship.

Questions for Contemplation and Discussion:

1. Make it a point to ask your spouse which part of the year is most difficult for him or her.
2. How will you communicate to your spouse that you are giving him or her the authority over your body?
3. What will you tell your spouse you need today? How confident are you that you'll get it? Take the risk and ask.

My Guy is Awesome!
Intimacy
Day 1
Song of Songs 2:16

What about your spouse first attracted you? How much of that attraction was directly a part of his or her life in sport? Some people are attracted to a person's role or even to how the person looks in sporting gear. How strong is the value of that initial attraction as the relationship matures?

The book of Hebrew poetry titled Song of Songs contains this simple thought in chapter two, verse sixteen, "My lover is mine, and I am his. He browses among the lilies." While the first part of this seems pretty simple, the latter is a little more obscure.

This woman speaks of her lover first as being hers. She is in possession of this man. This is the language of infatuation. "That's my boyfriend. He's a coach. He's wonderful." Sure, I'm his girl, but mostly he's mine. The whole "browsing among the lilies" thing is about cattle farming. This guy is so hot that his cattle eat flowers! "Those other guys' cattle eat grass, but not my guy. He's awesome!" "My guy's a state champion."

The early infatuation of young love is thrilling, full of wonder, and fraught with anxiety. It needs time to grow, mature, and move past the slightly selfish nature of, "My lover is mine." Enjoy these days of sweaty palms, lumps in the throat, and halting expressions of love. If you commit to each other, your love will mature.

Questions for Contemplation and Discussion:

1. Think about the moment in which you first saw your spouse. What was it that captured your attention? Have you shared that with him or her?
2. What about your lives in sport did you find most exciting in the early days of your relationship? Are they still there?
3. How has your relationship matured beyond those initial stages of selfish infatuation? What do you now find most attractive about your spouse?

Coaches are Nomads
Intimacy
Day 2
Genesis 2:24

What are some of the things you had to leave behind to be a part of this coaching family? How did those sacrifices affect the depth of commitment you have with your spouse? Take a moment to recall the conversations, the sleepless nights, and the fearful days of making still another move to continue as a coaching family. God knows that leaving the familiar to bond with one's spouse is a key part of loving intimacy. It has been that way since the beginning.

In Genesis chapter two, verse twenty-four, we read about the creation of man and woman. There it says, "This explains why a man leaves his father and mother and is joined to his wife, and the two are united into one." Without leaving the familiar and comfortable, there is no unified intimacy for a couple.

Coaching families are better acquainted with this process than most couples, as a career in coaching usually means frequent moves. The marriages that survive this process are usually rock solid and find they have an unusually strong bond of intimacy.

Husbands, take the risk to leave the comfort of the familiar to make the union you have with your wife all it can be.

She's worth it. Wives, go along with his nomadic spirit if it helps him to become the man God has called him to be. He's worth it. Coaching family, get out the moving boxes again; if God is leading you to this place, it will be worth it and you will be at your best.

Questions for Contemplation and Discussion:

1. When you think about what you have left behind to be a coaching family, what has been most costly? What has been most rewarding?
2. Which of the moves you have made during your career do you now regret? How will you talk with your spouse about that?
3. How has your nomadic lifestyle in coaching strengthened your bond of intimacy? How has it hindered your relationship? What needs to be adjusted?

I am Yours
Intimacy
Day 3
Song of Songs 6:3

When did you first become identified with your spouse? Are you sometimes referred to as, "Mrs. Coach," or do people say, "He's the coach's husband?" In our culture this happens most commonly when a bride on her wedding day changes her surname to that of her husband. Solomon wrote about this sort of intimate identification in a beautiful book of Hebrew poetry.

Song of Songs chapter six, verse three reads, "I am my lover's, and my lover is mine. He browses among the lilies." More cattle talk, we get it. He's a cool guy. Something has changed, however, in this young lady's speech. Earlier she said, "My lover is mine," but now she starts with, "I am my lover's." Their bond of love has grown past infatuation, and now she fully identifies herself with this man.

As relationships develop and intimacy grows, we become more and more identified with the one our soul loves. Early on a man may push back when referred to as "the coach's boyfriend," but as their bond grows, he's happy to be identified with her. Most coaches' wives are pleased to be, "Mrs. Coach," even when he's being criticized by the knuckleheads in the bleachers.

Commit deeply to each other. Identify yourselves, each with the other. This is an important part of growing a deep, intimate, loving relationship.

Questions for Contemplation and Discussion:

1. When did you first begin to be identified with your spouse? How did that change your relationship?
2. How do you respond when people identify you with your spouse rather than by something about you individually?
3. What are the traits in your spouse you wish you possessed? Take some time today to share those thoughts and express your admiration for him or her.

No Longer Two But One
Intimacy
Day 4
Mark 10:6-9

What are some factors that tear at the intimacy of your marriage? You're probably thinking about long work hours, frequent travel, constant distractions, and moving boxes. In what ways does it seems God has permanently knit your hearts together? I hope you are thinking about faithful love, expressions of commitment, intimate gazes into the other's eyes, and whispers in the ear. Such is the stuff of intimacy and bonding that stands the test of time and even coaching sport.

In the gospel of Mark, Jesus quotes Moses and takes things one step further. In chapter ten, verses six through nine we read, "But 'God made them male and female' from the beginning of creation. 'This explains why a man leaves his father and mother and is joined to his wife, and the two are united into one.' Since they are no longer two but one, let no one split apart what God has joined together."

Jesus has strong words for anyone or anything that would come between a husband and his wife. He says that it is God who has joined them together, and they are no longer two but one. He quotes Moses' account of the creation and goes one step beyond with his warning to not separate the intimate bond of a married couple.

Jesus' warning should lead us to evaluate the factors surrounding our coaching family that could cause us to split apart. Let's take some time to look closely at these things and make the needed adjustments to protect our bond of love and commitment.

Husband and wife, you are no longer two but one. Let nothing in heaven, on earth, or from the very pits of hell separate you. God continues to join you together, day by day. Guard your relationship.

Questions for Contemplation and Discussion:

1. What are the daily disruptors of intimacy and communication in your marriage?
2. What adjustments can be made to put away the factors that would separate your bond of intimacy and love?
3. What is your game plan for building your coaching family's unity?

Intimate Love is Its Own Reward
Intimacy
Day 5
Song of Songs 7:10

Have you come to a time in your life where your relationship with your spouse is its own reward? Do you still need all the trappings of the sporting life to keep your interest, or have you grown to love your spouse more deeply and intimately? Sadly, we all know people whose marriages have crumbled as soon as the player or coach was no longer in the sport. A marriage characterized by mature love and intimacy possesses something the merely infatuated and newly identifying lovers cannot even imagine.

Solomon wrote about mature love in Song of Songs chapter seven, verse ten. There it reads, "I am my lover's, and he claims me as his own." Now this woman has nothing to say about browsing among lilies. Neither does she make a claim of possession of her lover. She simply says, "I am my lover's." Selfless and content, she now is.

Further, she says, "he claims me as his own." Amazingly, she finds the true reward of this relationship is the bond of love and intimacy itself. She is no longer impressed by the external trappings of her lover; it is him that her soul loves. His claiming her as his own thrills her heart and brings joy to her soul.

Think about the oldest coaching couples you know. They don't look like they did in their youth. They don't do the exciting things they did as a young couple. They don't need to. Their bond of love and intimacy now finds the relationship is its own reward. This is the goal. Toward this intimate love we must all persevere.

Questions for Contemplation and Discussion:

1. Take a moment today to talk with your spouse about some of those long-enduring Christian coaching couples. What do you admire about them?
2. Think about a time you and your spouse can get together with one of those older coaching couples to talk about how they made their love last for so long. Set a date.
3. Make time to affirm your life long commitment to your spouse. Set your course toward a lifetime of love that has your intimate bond of love as its own reward.

Go To Work

Run—Leading a Busy Lifestyle
Day 1
Proverbs 14:23

How do you view the profession of coaching sport? Is it just a job to do? Is it something nobler? How should we view this calling if we are the spouse of a coach? How do we measure success?

Proverbs 14:23 informs our discussion with these words, "Work brings profit, but mere talk leads to poverty." Simple and direct, the proverb separates the value of work from the futility of empty talk.

Coaching is a noble profession. Being the spouse of a coach is also noble and significant. Your work together is of immense value to all those you influence. Your work leads to profit, not just in terms of money or victories, but in the development of the people you coach. Success is defined in terms of personal growth, skill development, building character, and transforming lives. Your work brings profit. Stay at it.

Mere talk leads to poverty. Those in the coaching profession, and even their spouses, who merely talk are quickly exposed and are soon dismissed. Rather than working productively, they chatter on with nothing to show from their hours with the team. Their verbal folly leads to empty lives and little influence.

I would challenge you, coach and spouse, to work diligently at your profession. Put in the necessary hours, sharpen your skills, and develop your career. There is profit in all such work. Beware the ones who only talk, as their empty babble will end in their own poverty.

Questions for Contemplation and Discussion:

1. How would you describe your view of coaching? Is it more like a profession, a job, or an avocation?
2. As a coach's spouse, how do you perceive coaching? Is it a noble profession, a way to pay the family's bills, or a pain in the neck?
3. How would your marriage and family life be affected if you approached coaching as "the family business?"

Go Recruit
Run—Leading a Busy Lifestyle
Day 2
Matthew 4:19-20

Think of the greatest recruiter with whom you have coached. Then consider how you went about recruiting your spouse. A dear coaching friend of mine, less than impressive in appearance, boasts of his recruiting ability by pointing to his very lovely bride. He says, "You think I can't recruit? Look at my wife!" Let's watch a master recruiter at work in today's scripture.

In Matthew's gospel chapter four, verse nineteen, he writes, "Jesus called out to them, 'Come follow me, and I will show you how to fish for people.' And they left their nets at once and followed him." Jesus is a tremendous recruiter. He made one call, and they were signed.

Whether you coach for a high school, a university, a professional club, or a recreational league, there is recruiting to be done. In some cases that requires many hours of travel, hundreds of phone calls, letters, text messages and more. All these factors can put a strain on a coaching family.

A wise coach will continue to recruit his or her spouse, well after their wedding day. The same pursuit that wins us the best players is required to keep the passion in our marriages. Make the extra visit. Call and text your spouse as often as you would a prized recruit. "Come follow me."

Whether coach or spouse, speak winsomely toward your love. Call him or her to, "Come follow me." Commit this day and every day to living a life of love with your number one recruit.

Questions for Contemplation and Discussion:

1. Think of the greatest recruiter with whom you have coached. What did that person do to recruit so effectively?
2. How did you go about recruiting your spouse when you were dating?
3. How was, "come follow me," expressed when your marriage proposal was made?

Go to Practice
Run—Leading a Busy Lifestyle
Day 3
Colossians 3:23

How do you approach training and practice sessions? Are they activities to be endured, or are they something more for you? Do you sense that your players reflect your attitude toward practice and training? Is practice any different in tone or intensity when the head coach is not watching? The answers to such questions will reveal a lot about us.

In the Apostle Paul's letter to his friends in Colossae, he writes in chapter three, verse 23, "Work willingly at whatever you do, as though you were working for the Lord rather than for people." Paul's admonition is clear and simple. Rather than seeing our work as primarily for our supervisor, our employer, or even the sport, he calls us to work as if the Lord Jesus Himself is the one to whom we directly report.

This is an attitude transforming approach for the coach and the coach's spouse. If we lace up our shoes, drape the whistle around our neck, and drive to practice with our minds conscious that we are going to coach for the Lord Jesus, everything about us is focused on honoring Him. Our view of the time spent looks more like an investment than a waste. Our work in every facet of coaching is more a matter of worship than drudgery. It's done for Him, not for people.

Please adopt Paul's attitude toward your work. Your attitude of such devotion consecrates coaching and makes it a holy vocation. Your respect for your spouse's life of coaching leads to a shared investment in all those impacted by this God-honoring labor. It is the Lord Christ you serve as you lead your coaching family. He is pleased with your faithful service.

Questions for Contemplation and Discussion:

1. Which of these would best describe your approach to daily practice and training?
    a. I can't wait until it's over.
    b. I can't wait to get there!
    c. I hope the head coach isn't there today.
    d. I am privileged to coach for the Lord Jesus.
2. How do you pray to prepare yourself for each day's practice?
3. Who is most helpful to your consecration of training and practice as matters of worship? What does that person do that's so helpful?

Go to the Game
Run—Leading a Busy Lifestyle
Day 4
1 Corinthians 9:24-25

When you think about competition, what images come to mind? Whose faces do you see? How similar is your spouse's view of competition? Would your view of competition be better described as beautiful or vulgar? Do you see it as profane or sacred?

When writing to his friends in Corinth, the Apostle Paul uses athletic competition as a metaphor for Christian living in chapter nine, verses 24 and 25. There he writes, "All athletes are disciplined in their training. They do it to win a prize that will fade away, but we do it for an eternal prize." The Apostle speaks of discipline and winning prizes, both temporal and eternal. This is the essence of coaching life.

The best athletes, and coaches for that matter, are disciplined or self-controlled in their training and during competition. We have all seen those who are out of control as they train and compete. They seldom win prizes of any sort. Competition and training are at their best when they are enhanced by a disciplined approach.

The homes of most coaches are graced by a wide array of trophies, rings, medals, ribbons, and plaques. They are prized memorials to days of excellence in competition. If one looks just beyond the shiny objects, the more enduring rewards of coaching life are also on display.

Post-game photos with a player, thank you notes, sideline passes from important competitions, mementoes from an important victory on the road and many more prizes of significance are also there. These items evoke memories of relationships, breakthroughs in life transformation, and moments of personal growth for those embraced by the coaching family. These are just some of the enduring prizes we possess.

When our coaching family is a part of the Lord Jesus' transformation of lives, the prizes are even more significant and are eternal in nature. Let's pursue all these prizes; those temporal, enduring, and eternal. They're worth all the disciplined training and competition.

Questions for Contemplation and Discussion:

1. What images and faces come to mind when you think of competition?
2. When do you think you come close to the edge of losing control when you compete?
3. What are some of your most cherished prizes from sport?
4. Share some of the most cherished relationships in your coaching family.

Go on Vacation
Run—Leading a Busy Lifestyle
Day 5
Mark 6:30-32

Coaching is a consuming lifestyle for the entire family. It chews up hours, energy, attention, and emotion, and it squeezes the margins of our lives. How can we build in time for family that refreshes our souls and replenishes our love for each other?

The Lord Jesus, during the three years of his ministry on earth was certainly busy. He had a short time to reveal God's will, accomplish His plan, and equip those who would further His mission. His approach to rest and rejuvenation is described in Mark chapter six, verses 30 through 32. There we read, "The apostles returned to Jesus from their ministry tour and told him all they had done and taught. Then Jesus said, 'Let's go off by ourselves to a quiet place to rest awhile.' He said this because there were so many people coming and going that Jesus and his apostles didn't even have time to eat. So they left by boat for a quiet place, where they could be alone."

The busyness of Jesus' life with the apostles was squeezing them harshly, so Jesus took action. He took them away from all the noise and commotion to rest. Twice, the text mentions that he sought a quiet place for them. He called them aside to rest and be alone.

Our coaching families should take note. Our families need to occasionally get away from the noise and commotion of our normal lives to somewhere quiet, to rest, and be alone. We need these moments, whether an hour over coffee with our spouse, a weekend away, a family vacation, or a sabbatical from work. We need the quiet, rest, and solitude to reflect, to reconnect with loved ones, and renew the bonds of devotion.

The challenge today is to be as responsive as Jesus was. Seek and schedule a time to say to your coaching family, "Let's go off by ourselves to a quiet place to rest awhile."

Questions for Contemplation and Discussion:

1. What about your coaching family life is consuming your time, energy, and attention?
2. How well do you schedule rest and recovery into your weekly agenda? Give yourself a grade: A, B, C, D, or F.
3. When and where will you take your coaching family away for some quiet and rest?

Why?

Throw—Communicating Effectively
Day 1
Isaiah 61:1

A number of years ago I was given a copy of the book, *Season of Life*, by Jeffrey Marx. The book chronicles the life transformation of Coach Joe Ehrmann. I found it to be deeply touching and of tremendous value, and I gave several copies to my coaching friends. Joe's heart piercing question for coaches is, "Why do you coach?" To contemplate that question and communicate it effectively is a powerful tool for a coaching family.

Similarly, the prophet Isaiah writes about his "Why" in Isaiah chapter 61, verse one. There we read, "The Spirit of the Sovereign Lord is upon me, for the Lord has anointed me to bring good news to the poor. He has sent me to comfort the brokenhearted and to proclaim that captives will be released and prisoners will be freed."

Isaiah served as he did because God had called and anointed him to bring good news, to comfort, and proclaim freedom. His transformational purpose statement was clear and powerful.

Coaching families are in a position similar to Isaiah's. God has chosen and anointed you to communicate a powerful message to those you lead. Speak good news to the disheartened and confused. Speak comfort to those broken by life. Proclaim freedom to those in chains of pain, guilt, addiction, and deceit.

You may find that you best communicate your "Why?" as a couple. Your coaching family may be the best expression of your transformational purpose, as you live, love, and communicate with those around you.

Questions for Contemplation and Discussion:

1. What would you say if someone asked you, "Why do you coach?"
2. On a 1 – 10 scale, how strongly do you sense that God has called and anointed you to coach? (1 = slightly, 10 = powerfully)
3. Describe some ways your coaching family can both communicate and demonstrate your calling to be God's messengers in sport.

What?

Throw—Communicating Effectively
Day 2
1 Timothy 1:5

When you approach a new season with your team, how clearly do you express your goals? How are they defined? Are your goals described by numbers of wins, scoring averages, tournament appearances, and championships? Are there other sorts of goals worth pursuing?

The Apostle Paul and I would like to challenge your whole coaching family with a goal of an entirely different kind. In his first letter to his protégé, Timothy, in chapter one, verse five, Paul wrote, "The purpose of my instruction is that all believers would be filled with love that comes from a pure heart, a clear conscience, and genuine faith."

Paul clearly states the goal for his coaching of Timothy. As wise coaches do, he lays out his expectations in a simple and direct manner.

We would do well to follow Paul's example when communicating our goals, both with our teams and with our families. Let's lead them to be filled with love. Let's ensure that such love comes from a pure heart, rather than one tainted by mixed motives. Let's guard the love we have for our teams and families by maintaining a clear conscience instead of being crushed by guilt.

Finally, let's have our love fueled by a genuine faith in Christ Jesus. Such faith produces a love much deeper than mere emotion.

Let's set some goals for our coaching families:
1. Sport achievement goals
2. Marriage goals
3. Family development goals
4. Lifetime and legacy goals

I pray your coaching family will achieve its goals with loving, pure hearts, clear consciences, and genuine faith.

Questions for Contemplation and Discussion:

1. What sorts of goals do you communicate with your teams? How do they respond?
2. What could be some goals for your family this year?
3. How can your coaching family make strides toward achieving the goals of pure hearted love, clear consciences, and genuine faith?

Who?

Throw—Communicating Effectively
Day 3
1 Corinthians 1:21-25

In your life of coaching, who are the most direct recipients of your communication? Obviously some of these include your team. Do you consider the ways you communicate with them? Is your manner of speaking the most effective way to develop players?

The Apostle Paul was a very effective communicator and we are privileged to read from his letters to the church at Corinth. In the first letter at chapter one, verses 21 through 25, we read, "Since God in his wisdom saw to it that the world would never know him through human wisdom, he has used our foolish preaching to save those who believe. It is foolish to the Greeks, who seek human wisdom. So when we preach that Christ was crucified, the Jews are offended and the Gentiles say it's all nonsense. But to those called by God to salvation, both Jews and Gentiles, Christ is the power of God and the wisdom of God. This foolish plan of God is wiser than the wisest of human plans, and God's weakness is stronger than the greatest of human strength."

Paul cuts through the cultural biases of both Greeks and Jews as he proclaims God's wisdom and strength in the sacrifice of Jesus Christ for the salvation of those who believe.

He acknowledges the natural bent of both groups and says the message of Christ Jesus is superior to their objections.

For coaches to communicate well they have to acknowledge and adjust to the cultural changes they encounter among their players. For coaching families to communicate well with their children and those in their communities, they have to be able to surf the waves of culture.

Your speech, your relationship with your spouse, your parenting, all of your life is full of God's wisdom and strength. Whether speaking of the team's values, the program's culture, one's family convictions, or the gospel of Jesus, we must find ways to cut through the cultural biases and communicate clearly with each one concerned.

Questions for Contemplation and Discussion:

1. With whom will you be communicating today?
2. Are you speaking as clearly and effectively as you would like? What do you find most challenging in this process?
3. How do you communicate your values for sport, family, and faith in Christ?

Where?
Throw—Communicating Effectively
Day 4
Acts 1:8

On whom do you perceive you have influence? You may first think of players, but also consider coaching colleagues, friends, family, sports fans, and even media. How widely do you suppose your influence is felt?

Jesus had some insight about the ripple effect of influence to share with his apostles, and he spoke of it in the book of Acts in chapter one, verse eight. There we read, "But you will receive power when the Holy Spirit comes upon you. And you will be my witnesses, telling people about me everywhere—in Jerusalem, throughout Judea, in Samaria, and to the ends of the earth." With an image of concentric circles of expanding influence, Jesus fuels the vision of his apostles.

These men had traveled through Jerusalem, Judea, and Samaria, but they were now challenged to believe their influence would ripple across the world to the ends of the earth. This had to turn their minds upside down. They had been simple fishermen, tax collectors, and men of other less than influential occupations. Now their leader says they will tell people about him all over the world.

If you were to suddenly have the ability to see the reach of your influence as a coaching family, I would imagine you would be similarly overwhelmed. Count your influence with those you encounter daily and multiply that by the number of years you will have in coaching. Exponentially compound that calculation by multiple generations of those influenced, and we may be approaching the impact of your life as a coaching family.

It is the very nature of coaching to have influence. That influence and its ripples of effect can be very helpful, or it can be very harmful. The quality of your influence will be determined by the nature of your heart. The good news is that a heart transformed by the power of God has the capacity to influence lives even beyond the grave. Our influence, as energized by the Holy Spirit, makes an impact locally, regionally, nationally, and even globally.

Questions for Contemplation and Discussion:

1. Make a list of the people, teams, and families with which you have influence.
2. How many people do you suppose your coaching family encounters in any given week?
3. How can you as a coaching family ensure your influence is of greatest benefit to those you love and serve?

When?

Throw—Communicating Effectively
Day 5
Matthew 10:7-8

As your life as a coaching family rolls along, what characterizes your central message? If someone was to simply observe your life, what would they say your life is about? What message do you suppose Jesus led his team to share as they walked around Palestine?

Matthew ten records Jesus' instructions for his team as they were sent out. In verses seven and eight we read these words, "Go and announce to them that the Kingdom of Heaven is near. Heal the sick, raise the dead, cure those with leprosy, and cast out demons. Give as freely as you have received." This was to be their daily assignment. Everywhere, every day, with everyone.

That's a pretty heavy message for a group to walk about sharing with people. It's a pretty tall order to heal sick people, raise dead people, cleanse lepers, and cast out demonic powers. That was exactly what Jesus called them to do.

Your calling as a coaching family is similar, but written in different language. You deal daily with people who are sin-sick and broken. Many under your influence are emotionally and spiritually dead, in desperate need of new life. Some people exist in the shadows of society like lepers. Still others around you are bound by destructive and powerful forces. Ours is a broken and despairing world, but we have a powerful and hopeful message to share.

Jesus' final injunction for his team is important to the process. "Give as freely as you have received." The power to carry Jesus' message and demonstrate his authority is freely given to us so that we may share it broadly. These rather common men were sent into a broken world with an uncommon measure of God's authority and power. So are we.

Let's make the message of our coaching families "the Kingdom of Heaven is near." Let's demonstrate the grace and mercy of Jesus by dealing effectively with the world's ills, its death, its despair, and its sin shackles. We have freely received; let's freely give.

Questions for Contemplation and Discussion:

1. What would you say is the central message of your life as a coaching family?
2. When do your best opportunities to share Jesus' message tend to appear?
3. How does your coaching family deal with people who are compromised by disease, death, social scorn, or life-controlling behaviors?

Home
Field—Dealing with Problems and Crises
Day 1
Ephesians 5:33-6:4

Every coaching family has to deal with problems and crises. Hopefully they don't occur often or repeatedly, but we should expect them to arise occasionally. Is there a prescription for problems? Is there a cure for the crises we encounter?

While there is no way to inoculate a family from these matters, there is good instruction for a wise, relational approach. It is found in Paul's letter to the church in Ephesus in chapter five verses 33 through chapter six, verse four. There we find this wisdom, "So again I say, each man must love his wife as he loves himself, and the wife must respect her husband. Children, obey your parents because you belong to the Lord, for this is the right thing to do. 'Honor your father and mother.' This is the first commandment with a promise: If you honor your father and mother, 'things will go well for you, and you will have a long life on the earth.' Fathers, do not provoke your children to anger by the way you treat them. Rather, bring them up with the discipline and instruction that comes from the Lord."

Most people hear these as an outline for family life. After a couple of decades of life in sport, I see them through the prism of problems and crises that can arise for a coaching family. These verses give some guidelines for how to relate to people in the midst of such issues.

With your spouse, demonstrate love and respect. This puts us both in a good posture for dealing with problems. With your parents, obey and honor them. This attitude makes the crisis easier to manage. With your children, nurture and instruct them. To do less will likely provoke them and only amplify the problem.

To establish our relationships in the home on the best possible foundation is the wisest approach to problems and crises, even before they raise their ugly heads. Build your home with love, respect, honor, obedience, nurture, and instruction. Neither problems nor crises can successfully assault such a coaching family.

Questions for Contemplation and Discussion:

1. What sorts of problems or crises does your coaching family most often encounter?
2. Which of these best describes how you normally approach such issues:
    a. Run and hide?
    b. Confront them head on?
    c. Hope they go away?
    d. Band together and deal with their causes?
3. How well do you think your family embodies the relational qualities in the Bible text?

Work

Field—Dealing with Problems and Crises
Day 2
Hebrews 10:24

What most motivates your coaching colleagues? Where are the motivational buttons on your players? What brings out the best in your spouse? When you ask your children about homework or assigned tasks, how do you keep them engaged?

The writer of the biblical book of Hebrews understood that motivation is not a one-size-fits-all proposition. He writes about it in chapter ten, verse 24. There we read, "Let us think of ways to motivate one another to acts of love and good works." This simple sentence is loaded with key verbs and nouns for our instruction.

He instructs us to "think of ways to motivate." This implies that we must consider there may be multiple different ways to motivate the people around us. We are all wired differently. Some may be motivated by reward, others by encouragement, others by challenge, still others by fear, and some by the promise of a promotion or a financial bonus. What is it with you? What most motivates your spouse?

A few other key words are, "acts of love and good works." Some folks are plenty motivated but not to acts of love and good works. What are the ways you can best move your players toward love and good works? How do we motivate our family members to be their best?

The challenge for each of us is to carefully consider all those we lead and discern the best ways to lead them to act lovingly and serve each other. This makes for great teamwork on the field of competition, and it makes for a wonderful coaching family.

Questions for Contemplation and Discussion:

1. What have you observed to best motivate those with whom you coach?
2. What motivates your family members to be their best?
3. What would you tell your spouse is the number one way to motivate you to acts of love and good works?

Team
Field—Dealing with Problems and Crises
Day 3
1 Peter 5:2-3

How do you perceive the relationships you have with those you coach? Does it look like a boss to employee relationship? Maybe it's more like teacher to pupil. For some of us it may be a mentor to protégé relationship. Some coaches approach it like master to slave. The way we perceive our relationships will have a direct bearing on how we approach problem solving and crisis management.

Peter, the Apostle, spoke of a shepherd to sheep relationship as he wrote to his friends in his first letter, in chapter five, verses two and three. There we read, "Care for the flock that God has entrusted to you. Watch over it willingly, not grudgingly - not for what you will get out of it, but because you are eager to serve God. Don't lord it over the people assigned to your care, but lead them by your own good example." Coaching families, like pastors, are to care for, and watch over those entrusted to their care, leading them by good example.

Coach, to care for your flock means that you will know each one personally. That takes time and attention. Watch over them; protect them from harm. Lead by your good example; show them how to live. Some of this is done at practice and on game day. Much more of it is done when they observe how you love and nurture your family.

Rather than lording it over them, intimidating them into good behavior and excellent performance, when you care for, watch over, and lovingly lead them you will produce the best in and for them.

Coaching family, be wise and caring shepherds for the flock God has entrusted to you. Not for what you will get out of it but because you are eager to serve God.

Questions for Contemplation and Discussion:

1. Which of these best describes how you perceive the relationships you have with those you coach?
      a. Boss to employee?
      b. Teacher to pupil?
      c. Mentor to protégé?
      d. Master to slave?
2. How do you care for, watch over, and lead your team?
3. How can your spouse be helpful as your coaching family shepherds the flock God has entrusted to your care?

Extended Family
Field—Dealing with Problems and Crises
Day 4
I Timothy 5:8

Have you ever seen people abandon members of their extended family when they have fallen on hard times? Issues like bankruptcy, addiction, moral failure, and even imprisonment can cause some of us to run away from the compromised family member. Most of us will encounter one, if not all, of these issues in our extended families, among our players, or with coaching colleagues at some point.

The Apostle Paul has some very direct and blunt language for such situations in his first letter to his protégé, Timothy, in chapter five, verse eight. That verse reads, "But those who won't care for their relatives, especially those in their own household, have denied the true faith. Such people are worse than unbelievers."

Did you have someone's face come to mind as you read that passage? In this clear admonition, the apostle ties our care for extended family directly to our faith in Christ. He also states that to fail in this responsibility makes our behavior worse than those who don't even know Jesus. The most heathen people you know care for their families. Shall we not?

We must not let the lies of self-preservation creep into our minds, as if our reputations are somehow tarnished by embracing the broken and sin-stained among our family members. Paul's admonition would be to run directly to their aid, not away from their weakness and pain.

Coaching family, we are challenged to care deeply for those in our extended family whose lives are broken. Let's be the ones who demonstrate Jesus' love, grace, and mercy.

Questions for Contemplation and Discussion:

1. When has your coaching family encountered such a situation in your extended family?
2. Has something like that happened in a team or among coaching colleagues? What happened?
3. How did you deal with these issues?
4. Are you pleased with your response? What would you do differently now?

Community
Field—Dealing with Problems and Crises
Day 5
Titus 3:1-2

How does your coaching family relate to the broader community in which you live? Do you feel well connected with it or do you live in a sort of sporting community bubble? Often those in the coaching profession live with a widely different set of values and expectations than those in the general population. This leads to some distance and alienation and can even create problems.

The Apostle Paul, when writing to his colleague, Titus, gave him some wise counsel about dealing with the broader community in which he lived and served. Chapter three, verses one and two of Titus read like this, "Remind the believers to submit to the government and its officers. They should be obedient, always ready to do what is good. They must not slander anyone and must avoid quarreling. Instead, they should be gentle and show true humility to everyone."

Though surrounded by a community of people with a vastly different value system to these early believers, Paul encouraged Titus to lead them wisely. This counsel certainly helped them avoid a number of problems and crises.

It is wise to submit to the government and its officers. Obedience and good behavior is seldom punished. It is wise to avoid slander and quarrels. Social media and text messaging has only amplified this wisdom. It is wise to be gentle and humble in our relationships. To arrogantly push our way around is neither winsome nor effective in solving problems.

Even while your coaching family and your coaching colleagues live with a much different set of values and expectations from the general community, as you follow Paul's counsel you can be confident you will have a wise approach to problems and crises.

Questions for Contemplation and Discussion:

1. What are some of the values and expectations your sporting community hold that are far different from the broader community?
2. In what situations do you find it most difficult to submit to the government and its officers?
3. How does your family demonstrate gentleness and humility in relationship with people outside your sporting community?

Players
Hit for Power—Making a Strong Impact
Day 1
2 Timothy 4:1-2

Think about the coaches who have had the greatest impact upon your life. Where did the moments of strong influence occur? Some surely were at practice or on game day. You may remember a talk in the classroom or a chat in the coach's office. Those most important days may have occurred away from sport or even in the coach's home. The wisest among us are ready to make a significant impact, regardless of the season or situation.

The Apostle Paul understood this dynamic and wrote about it in his second letter to his protégé, Timothy, in chapter four, verses one and two. There we read, "I solemnly urge you in the presence of God and Christ Jesus, who will someday judge the living and the dead when he comes to set up his Kingdom: Preach the word of God. Be prepared, whether the time is favorable or not. Patiently correct, rebuke, and encourage your people with good teaching."

Paul's solemn instruction to Timothy was to be prepared to make an impact at any time, on any day, in any situation. He called him to patiently correct, rebuke, and encourage the people in his charge.

As a coaching family, your opportunity to make a significant impact will not likely get scheduled a week ahead of time. It could as easily occur in a moment of mind dulling mundanity as well as in a setting of excitement and exhilaration. The life changing conversation with a player could happen as you gather up gear after practice or it could appear as you celebrate a championship. The heart bonding chat with your son or daughter could take place as you carry out the trash or just before leaving for a homecoming dance.

Coaching family, as Paul exhorted Timothy, be prepared. Communicate correction, rebuke, and encouragement with great patience. In doing such you stand to make a strong impact that will affect those you lead, now and for generations to come.

Questions for Contemplation and Discussion:

1. Who are those coaches with greatest impact upon your life?
2. What did they do or say that so strongly affected you?
3. When have you had a similar moment to speak into the lives of others?
4. How will you prepare so that you are ready, whether the time is favorable or not?

Colleagues

Hit for Power—Making a Strong Impact
Day 2
Ephesians 4:1-2

Your role as a coaching family is a high calling from God. How well did that sentence settle in your mind? How strongly does it resonate in your heart? Is this role something you have come to embrace as a vocation, an expression of your devotion to God? Many of your colleagues see it through the lens of their stipend, while others view it through the eyes of God. Which are you?

In his letter to the church at Ephesus, in chapter four, verses one through three, the Apostle Paul strongly calls his friends to a high standard. There we read, "Therefore I, a prisoner for serving the Lord, beg you to lead a life worthy of your calling, for you have been called by God. Always be humble and gentle. Be patient with each other, making allowance for each other's faults because of your love." That's a challenging and direct standard for a group of people who live in a debaucherously pagan city.

We are similarly challenged today as coaching families. Our calling is from God, and we must lead a life worthy of our calling. Live worthy of it; don't defame it professionally or as a family. Be humble and gentle, putting away arrogance and intimidation. Be patient and unified as a coaching staff and as a coaching family.

Imagine the impact your coaching family can have with your colleagues and friends as your career stretches from months to years to decades. Only the Lord Jesus can grasp the breadth and depth of your Spirit-fueled influence.

To demonstrate these qualities in our coaching and in our family life is certainly worthy of our calling. Our love for each other carries these attitudes and behaviors to full fruition and pleases our Lord greatly.

Questions for Contemplation and Discussion:

1. When you read that first sentence, what sort of a reaction did it prompt in you?
2. Who are some coaching families that you perceive live with a sense of calling from God?
3. What are some facets of your coaching life that may not be worthy of your calling?
4. How will your love for the people you lead empower your patience with them?

Officials
Hit for Power—Making a Strong Impact
Day 3
Romans 13:1-2

Take a moment to recall some of your best and worst moments with sports officials. I would imagine the worst ones were quicker to come to mind. How shall we as a coaching family relate to the referees, officials, and umpires who arbitrate our competitions?

Before you slam the book down and stomp off, let's seek some wisdom from the Bible to shape our thoughts on this subject. In his letter to the church in Rome in chapter 13, verses one and two, the Apostle Paul writes, "Everyone must submit to governing authorities. For all authority comes from God, and those in positions of authority have been placed there by God. So anyone who rebels against authority is rebelling against what God has instituted, and they will be punished."

I hear you thinking, "Yeah, but you don't know our officials." Paul was writing in reference to the men who would soon order his execution. He says to submit to governing authorities, even the ones who can remove your head.

The point is obviously to submit to authority rather than rebel against it. We will not likely agree with every official's ruling or even with how he or she officiates. Paul's command is that we submit to the governing officials as we submit to God. Even when we don't understand what God is doing in our lives, we still submit. Let's give the officials, umpires, or referees the same latitude when we don't understand or agree with their rulings.

Imagine the impact your coaching family can have on the men and women who officiate your sport when you treat them with respect and submit willingly to their leadership. They are fully one third of each sporting contest. Let's give them the respect that comes with their God-given authority.

Questions for Contemplation and Discussion:

1. Which faces came to mind when you thought about your worst moments with an official?
2. Who did you think of when you recalled a good experience with an official?
3. How hard do you find it to submit to the officials on game day? (1 = no sweat. 10 = I can't stand it!)
4. How well does your coaching family submit to authority beyond the sporting world? (Police, city officials, taxing bodies, state and federal governments…)

Opponents
Hit for Power—Making a Strong Impact
Day 4
1 Corinthians 16:13-14

When you think about your opponents on the field of competition, do they seem more like friends or enemies? Are they worms to be crushed into the dirt or valued colleagues with whom to strive toward excellence? Your answer will reveal a lot about your heart.

Near the end of his first letter to the church at Corinth, the Apostle Paul wrote some brief, direct, pointed sentences that will challenge us all. In chapter 16, verses 13 and 14, we read his instructions, "Be on guard. Stand firm in the faith. Be courageous. Be strong. And do everything with love."

Let's think about each of these directives in relation to our lives in sport. "Be on guard." Not everyone in sport is honorable. Keep your guard up and protect your team. "Stand firm in the faith." Hold tightly to the values your faith provides. You are swimming upstream. "Be courageous." Compete fearlessly. "Be strong." Train and prepare to compete at your very best. "Do everything with love." Yes, even competition. Seek the best for all concerned. This brings out the best in sport, just as cheating and foul play defiles it.

When we follow Paul's leadership in our coaching responsibilities, and beyond them as we lead our families, we make a strong impact upon our opponents. Such impact breeds respect, loyalty, trust, and even love for each other.

Take a moment to dream about how good sport can be when its competitors love and respect each other. They strive together to achieve their highest level of excellence, joy, and fulfillment. Let's pursue that goal. When you go out to compete, "Be on guard. Stand firm in the faith. Be courageous. Be strong. And do everything with love."

Questions for Contemplation and Discussion:
1. Who are the opponents you most strongly respect? Why do you feel that way?
2. What are the factors in your sport for which you most often have to be on guard?
3. Have you ever experienced a sporting event in which the competitors loved and respected each other? What was the outcome for those who experienced it?

Fans

Hit for Power—Making a Strong Impact
Day 5
John 10:16

For whom do you feel most responsible as a coaching family? You probably thought of your spouse, your kids, your team, your coaching colleagues and support staff. Did you think of the spectators? How much responsibility does a coach have for the alternatingly fawning and cursing crowds of sports fans?

Jesus had a solid team of twelve that traveled with him, a set of one hundred twenty that were a little more distant, and literally thousands who crowded around him daily. We get a feel for how he saw these disparate groups in John's gospel in chapter ten, verse 16. There it reads, "I have other sheep, too, that are not in this sheepfold. I must bring them also. They will listen to my voice, and there will be one flock with one shepherd."

Jesus was a master at dealing wisely with groups of widely varying levels of commitment. While speaking directly with his disciples, he would speak in parables with those less committed and even more obliquely with his opponents. Here he speaks of himself as a shepherd who has not only this set of sheep, but others not in this fold. His language is broad enough to leave room for interpretation by all those hearing him.

Wise coaches speak very directly with their coaching colleagues and their competitors. They speak differently with the media, just a few steps outside the sheepfold, and even more obliquely when speaking with fans.

Coaching families who understand Jesus best know that there is a measure of responsibility for those following their teams. It's not the same for those in this sheepfold, but how we speak, gesture, and lead our families is observed by dozens, hundreds, or many thousands. Coach, they will listen to your voice as surely as Jesus' sheep do.

Questions for Contemplation and Discussion:

1. On a scale of 1 to 10, how much responsibility do you feel for your team's fans? (1 = none, 10 = strong responsibility)
2. How do you vary your communication between those in your sheepfold and those outside?
3. How conscious are you during competition of all the sets of eyes that are on you? What does that awareness lead you to do?

Twenties
Hit for Average—Loving for a Lifetime
Day 1
Proverbs 16:9

Many coaching families begin with a wedding during their twenties. This is a decade full of major decisions; what to do for a living, where to live, whether to marry, whom to marry, whether to have children.

King Solomon lends us some wise counsel in the book of Proverbs in chapter 16 and verse nine. There it says, "We can make our plans, but the Lord determines our steps." That seems pretty simple, but to live it out is a little more complex. Let's consider the implications for a coaching family.

It's a good thing to have a plan, and the proverb leaves us room to make plans. It's also a good thing to allow some wiggle room in our plan for the Lord to make course corrections. Most of us, when we're in our twenties, make plans for family and career, but we'd have to confess our vision is pretty blurry. The Lord has no such lack of clarity. He knows and is well prepared to direct our steps toward the fulfillment of His purposes and our joy.

Ask any coaching couple in their sixties how closely their path of family and career matches the plans they made as newlyweds. They will probably chuckle at the disparity and will surely marvel at the Lord's wisdom.

The coaching family in their twenties imagines that the map of their coaching life will be a straight line from point A to point B, always moving up and to the right. It is to our benefit that the Lord doesn't allow us such a path. He knows much of what we will need is not on the A to B straight line path. We gather much of the character, skills, knowledge, and wisdom we need for our arrival at point B, way off the path due to failure, betrayal, bad decisions, and even rebellion. The Lord determines our steps and will not fail to fully equip us.

During your twenties, trust the Lord to guide you through the major decisions, even if you can't see clearly and wonder where the path has gone. He is leading and will deliver you right on time.

Questions for Contemplation and Discussion:

1. What sorts of decisions were you making in your twenties? How many of those decisions worked out as you thought they would?
2. What are the major decisions you would like to have another shot at making?
3. How clearly can you see the Lord's hand in directing your steps as you look back on your twenties? Which course corrections did you resist at first?

Thirties
Hit for Average—Loving for a Lifetime
Day 2
Proverbs 22:29

During one's thirties, a coach tends to master his or her craft. This decade usually exponentially develops the coach's skill set, knowledge base, and personal network. Much of what was gathered in the twenties begins to be cast off in favor of a narrower set of goals and priorities. This process has implications for the whole coaching family.

King Solomon has some encouragement for the coaching family in its thirties. Proverbs chapter 22, verse 29 contains a vision fueling truth for the developing coaching family. There we read, "Do you see any truly competent workers? They will serve kings rather than working for ordinary people." Most coaches see themselves as far beyond "truly competent."

Coaches and their spouses are typically rather ambitious people. Their reach often exceeds their grasp, but not for long. You probably locked onto that second sentence when you saw it. Wouldn't you rather serve kings than work for ordinary people? Every thirty-something coach I know wants to be the king even more than to serve him.

The wisdom in the proverb for the coaching family is the assurance that the Lord sees your competence and will move on your behalf to put you in a role commensurate with your level of competence. Rather than working hard at self-promotion, work hard at your competence and trust God to promote you. He has a direct phone line to the kings of your sport and has plenty of influence to deliver you to the best possible place.

During your thirties, concentrate on being the competent worker. Let God move the heart of the king.

Questions for Contemplation and Discussion:

1. What are you beginning to master during the decade of your thirties?
2. What were some of the roles, activities, and interests you accumulated during your twenties that dropped in importance soon after turning thirty?
3. In what ways are you diligently building your coaching competence?

Forties
Hit for Average—Loving for a Lifetime
Day 3
2 Timothy 2:2

Coaches and their spouses in their forties often begin to multiply their particular successes, styles, habits, values, and skills into the lives of those coaching around them. This is altogether wise and proper. It is also well described in scripture.

In the Apostle Paul's second letter to his protégé, Timothy, in chapter two, verse two, he writes, "You have heard me teach things that have been confirmed by many reliable witnesses. Now teach these truths to other trustworthy people who will be able to pass them on to others." Paul describes the generational effect that he desired for Timothy to continue, and we see the same effect among our coaching colleagues, mentors, and protégés.

It is very common for coaches to talk together and discuss the "coaching tree" of one of their respected colleagues. Those coaches trace their lineage to a legendary coach as if it were their family tree. They speak of coaching's generational effect with a tone of reverence.

The decade of one's forties may have your coaching family's influence at its zenith. You have lots of energy, experience, and passion. Your spouse is deeply engaged, your kids are in the community, and you are a person in demand.

Coach, Paul and I would challenge you to give yourself away. The things you have learned from colleagues and mentors, teach them to other trustworthy coaches who will be able to pass them on to others.

For the coaching family in its forties, these are great times of powerful influence and rich relationships. Take full advantage of every moment by multiplying the best of your heart and soul into those around you.

Questions for Contemplation and Discussion:

1. What have you begun to multiply in others during your forties?
2. From whom did you learn some of the most transferable coaching values, skills, and knowledge you now possess?
3. Into whose lives are you now multiplying? Who else is on your radar for such multiplication?

Fifties
Hit for Average—Loving for a Lifetime
Day 4
Acts 28:30-31

Once a couple is in their sixth decade of life, they hit a whole new gear. Suddenly they are possessed of the wisdom, experience, knowledge, insight, and relationships to mentor effectively.

The closing verses of the book of Acts, Luke's account of early Church history written to his friend Theophilus, describe the Apostle Paul's life as a prisoner in Rome. In chapter 28, verses 30 and 31, we read, "For the next two years, Paul lived in Rome at his own expense. He welcomed all who visited him, boldly proclaiming the Kingdom of God and teaching about the Lord Jesus Christ. And no one tried to stop him." Ironically, in the prison where he was to be executed, Paul enjoyed the greatest freedom of his ministry as he spoke boldly and mentored widely.

Coaching families in their fifties can take a page from Paul's example as they approach their last decades of life with wisdom and rich relationships.

"He welcomed all who visited him." As Paul received Romans, Jews, prisoners, guards, believers and not-yet-believers, he was welcoming to all. Coaching families should also be welcoming.

"Boldly proclaiming." As Paul spoke boldly with those who visited him, so may the coaching family. They came to see him; they must want to know what he has to say. Ditto.

"No one tried to stop him." Paul's experience, his reputation, and his scars won him the authority and respect to speak freely. It's the same with the experienced coaching family. Your experience, your reputation, and even your scars from decades of coaching have won you the authority and respect to speak freely.

Sixty-something coaching family, you are in a powerfully strategic spot. You are equipped to mentor coaches and their families who are in their forties, their thirties, and their twenties. You are both immensely blessed and possessed of a massive responsibility. I pray you embrace both as fully as possible.

Questions for Contemplation and Discussion:

1. Who are some of the people seeking you out for advice and insight?
2. When and where are the best options for meeting to mentor them?
3. How boldly do you speak with them?
4. Do you feel the authority and respect you possess? Why or why not?

Sixties and Beyond
Hit for Average—Loving for a Lifetime
Day 5
Proverbs 17:6

Being a grandparent is a mystical and magical experience. From the moment the pregnancy is announced, the whole world changes and we desperately love and anxiously await this person we have yet to meet.

The biblical wisdom book of Proverbs contains a tremendous insight into the heart of a grandparent. In chapter 17, verse six we read, "Grandchildren are the crowning glory of the aged; parents are the pride of their children."

A coaching family that includes grandchildren is a marvelous thing. Grandparents wear the crown of glory their little ones provide with great pride and joy. It's amazing to watch tough-guy coach reduced to a quivering bowl of jelly as his newborn granddaughter arrives at practice. Focused, task driven grandmothers shut down every other person on the planet when their grandbabies are at hand.

Grandparents, the aged as described in the proverb, are now able to live in both halves of the scripture. They experience the crowning glory of their grandchildren, and they feel the joy of seeing their children as parents, the pride of the grandkids. To hear one's grandchildren scream, "Daddy!" when he walks in the house, is the very stuff of life. To watch one's daughter wiping the tears from her own child's cheek, deeply enriches the hearts of her parents.

If your coaching family now includes grandchildren, you are richly blessed. Wear that glorious crown with joy, and then watch your sons and daughters be the pride of their children. Such are the rewards of a faithful life. Enjoy every moment.

Questions for Contemplation and Discussion:

1. Do you remember the moment you learned you were to become grandparents? What did you feel? What did you say?
2. What do your grandchildren do that crowns your life?
3. What have you observed in your kids, now that they are parents, that makes them the pride of the grandkids?